Picnic Poetry

Stephen Kopel,
provisioner

Picnic Poetry

Kopel, Stephen, 1940-

Picnic Poetry

     a. witty b. wordplayful

     c. digestible humor

ISBN - 13: 978-0615581941

Library of Congress Control Number: 2011963236

First Edition

Printed in the United States of America

Picnic Poetry

Dedicated

to our cents of humor

worth big bucks

if piggy holds up your bank

Appetite for the audacious?

This picnic is for you!

PROVISIONS

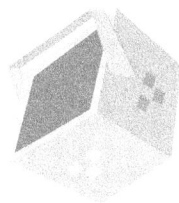

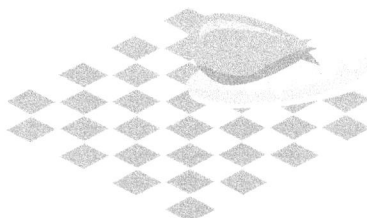

SIDES

EXTRA HELPINGS

CLEAN-UP

STARTERS

<u>Hops on a Harley</u>

Via ducked when
Heineken threw a party

thespians did a few lines,
Hashish played the heroine

baby carrots bawled when
the cell phoned -
Miranda reading her rights

Sofia's sofa collapsed
in a fit of giggles

plastic knives sliced
into debris so the

Swiss Army was never
called on to perform

stuck in traffic,
Zipper arrived late

Katz shaved his whiskers
so Lamm could lick his chops

a troupe of mice harmonized
with the cat's meow

and, the Grimm brothers
decided, finally, to
give up frowning

Aviary

To me, it seemed she was
no stranger on this train:
plucking dimples from her beaded bag,
cutting the deck with a butter knife,
persuading caboose sign a truce over gin

Was the baggage car visited by nuns
whose habits compelled them
to stand on ceremony, then,
fly en masse to the
closest gothic groin?

In their Pullman car,
acolytes shower in bath water
borrowed from the Pittsburg Psycho,
stealer of leather wallets confiscated
from every Broox brother who pedalled, yet,
never learned to handle the bars

That gin-rummied blond last seen
entering her contract's sunset clause,
did she climb out a rear window
begging pal Vertigo downhill fast?

And, who's the rotund conductor
hoping to get off a shot or two
while birds of a feather flock together?

Basic Training

First lieutenant leaves his toupee
prey for hipcats in spatz,
wolves in sheep's clothing, madhatters,
buried in the hamper

squad of grunts march a platoon
of ragtag, onionskinthin blankets,
sheets into whirlpools' sudsy
effluvium whose iron will wilts, now,
in the face of a ferocious detergent

smell that salt
in the smalls of backs..
nervous, trigger-happy
one-eyed jacks order
all patches off-duty,
the beauty of leave
is a shore of dinahs,
beer and burgers a buck,
fries on the house,
bald officer first up the ladder

Hold The Buns

in Munich,
intrigued by his vibrato,
I follow this famous
Faust into the sauna,
a mean stream of steam
pours out of an aria
he sweats to sing,
loosens his towel and
every well-placed vowel
drips with sarcasm

I figure soles can be
transfigured here..
capped and gowned, I graduate
to a higher realm of massage
confident that under my guidance,
together, we'll wrest a victory
from da feet

onstage in Hamburg, his manicured
voice nails the notes,
box sitters request hamburgers,
medium-rare, be served at the interval,
Patty Hearst hides in the balcony,
a Polish ham her escort,
twice-sliced in a sauerkraut mood

later, in Cologne,
before meeting Chanel at 5,
he charges Carmen's baby bull,
steals Escamillo's Cape of Good Hope
and slashed the rope
bringing down the curtain

in Berlin, threw back too many Weiss biers,
his final song a swan too lethargic to swim

Breighton boardwalk cafe this summer,
British bangers explode on tourists' tongues
and his broken voice-box barks orders
to our short short-order cook,
(a countertenor recently off the high seas),
while, I, still intrigued by his vibrato,
scrape-cleaning plastic plates,
continue to remove the salt from his wounds

Operatic

Norman, Druid priest,
retired, galled by
number-one wife's indiscretions,
sells his wooded parcel -
a grove populated by
towering bohemians,
Roman sentries up the creek,
Dubai Developers
his transfer agent and
tree trunks remover -
in exchange for a
well-maintained traditional
crenulated sand castle
all co-joined tangent to a
Rick Steves-recommended
caravansary and limo lot

a bitter separation feud,
one can see,
prompted by wife Norma's
unexplained infatuation
with horny balladeer Romano,
whose lyre, positioned
between strong thighs,

she strummed, she stroked,
even during moonless episodes
as her chorus followers
raised their voices in
feigned domestic harmonies while
scrubbing acorn-littered hearths,
collecting branches of the
main librarium and chiseling
in stone Stonehenge homilies

ah, battles between the ex's..
the cosmic itchery of sevens..

"Hexes on 'em both"
nods bewhiskered Elder,
solid as an oak

Ruiz, Darling

she flings another
cashmere sigh over
her Picasso shoulder

a tongue tattoo licks
her single mammary

all nine toes, dainty
thumb, soak in rosé

though she's long past
celebrating a romance
short on Cuban cigars,
rolls in the hay, flan

her left elbow,
outside the canvas,
awaits the painter's kiss

or brush off
as he steals
a Barcelona nap

Rack

Aphrodite,
in her nightie,
bid sturdy stag
do drag her, face
feigning fright,
to that place certain
to draw night's curtain,
thus, giving cover
to lovers' lust

That their rut
was next day's news
failed to amuse
deities of second rank
who viewed the prank
with much disdain,
ordering restraint
be coaxed into
the moral code

Cow Chorus

heroic notes bestir the air
measured chews, a perfunctory beat,
unify ungulates into a field of followers

one moo, multitude of moos,
quavers penetrate udders,
milker melodies slow filling

flatulence, variable pitch, resonates
evidence of devotional fervor,
this ordinary blessed bovinity singeth

Bull Boris,
believer in chorus interruptus,
notes a swelling approval,

paws the grass,
decides to conduct another morning pass

Retinowski

hungry for munchies,
frantic rabbit

chases after Alice,
scatterbrain palace thief,
whose holy camisole
keeps dropping carats
on Persian runners
stretched out on a
marble palisade
dreaming of marathons
in scenic Mandalay,
surf giving birth
to Dorothy Lamour,
sarong folded just right
practicing her habit
of advising each rabbit

to forget Alice,
shoot for Dallas
and the arms of
Madam Sarah Tonin

EU rose out of the Thames

No potato dumplings graduate today, though
Russet's SATs speak well of wide-eyed
devotion to grey matter, to matters at hand,
especially hands in work gloves, canvas,
top grade, made in the USA ready for labor,
mid-wifery, full-time or part, even handed out
at parties where carpenters from hard-knock
colleges polish their nails, measure, hammer,
bandsaw splintery instruments The Carpenters
donated, their final Nashville concert a
concerted effort to bring down the house -
walls, windows, roof in a free-fall
surreal Chagall collapse - domicile tenderized by
fans of term limits, a certain species of
termites masticating, gorging, digesting,
then, spitting phloem in a bluesgrassy,
brassy display of southern horsepitality
out to welcome UK tourists tired of pitching
horseshoes, tired of spud floaters at food
fairs, mired in more debt than mizzens have
massed, who wait in a friendly queue for
service with a mile to go for the tastiest
crow humble pie provides

Daze of the Week

Blue Munday, smelly and through with cigs,
tub-soaked her keel, then yelled "Abandon
Ship", the final chocochip tripping over
oars and a fancy leather loafer floating by

Carrying his speedos in a zippered pouch,
Ms Blue tossed an anchor to beach guard
Tom Tuesday hoping to hold him and his heat

Into bags burlapian and agape, collapsing
claptraps of Malaysian origin did on a
Wednesday wander

Turning Thursday around to confront a fracas,
metalmen welded complaints to iron beams, then,
bathed in a shower of sparks

Friday flooded the news with views salty,
even salient, leaving psychology perplexed
at apartment complexes under construction

Saturn and son Day faced off in the Garden of
Eattin' each grating like mad to further the
fad of welcoming cabbages from colleges,
sprouts from boarding schools

Bonjour

a cowherd cowered
alarmed by a tinker's bell,
daffydills in no laffy mood

losing its best line,
reduced to a mere
fraction of itself,
numerator
thumbs a jokes book

Tuileries bombast -
a feline invasion,
Company C dives in
the Gene Pool,
tails masted, squads
dogpaddle to the other side

Gardens balmblast -
everywhere petroleum jelly,
numerator smacked,
smeared below the line

cows masticate 'dills and,
past your eyes, tots
got the hots for milk

delivered to Notre Dame
whose organ awaits a
pedal pipe pusher packing notes
played as lullaby before
bedtime milkers hit the hay

drippy tabbies mewl,
fuel a rushed retreat
on this Parisian cattlefield
forcing a still photographer
slip out of her pose,
plant tripod squarely on
Gene Pool's muddy bottom

shutter speed slow..
escargot

race for the border

Collared

from the piedmont to the prairie,
Gary to the western coast,
our prayers pray to be heard
by hymns and by hers,

settle in bell towers of
peoples' steeples pointing the way
to the highway to heaven where
detour signs and potholes abound
leaving priests directing traffic
to cloud nine's lost and found,
and, if caught fingering a lucky foot,
can stand at ease and yell,
"Ah, men,
bring on benedictionaries."

Webster defining for his flock
the importance of carrying
the copy right..or, not at all

Mara Kesh

a stuck stocking tightens its grip
on thighology, mocking knees
exposed by a breeze through a Berber tent,
Abercrombie, on all fours,
stakes a claim for decency,
for the home office,
for Bedouins, barbered,
knickerbockered
in the back of Tata Vans

"Ta, ta, daddy," waves Amber,
daughter galloping over dunes,
overdoing her allegiance
to the company store,
adjusting garters that
loosen grips on thighs,
she sighs, though the size of her
Harry Winston is worth staking a claim for

and behind a hand-carved door,
the remainder of Berbers' beards -
fabled nesting sites for desert kites

Sinema

elevators refuse to rise before noon,
but, stairs lay down the carpet for early risers
who find the theater's box office agreeable to
approach unlike Matt Tress and Ms Box Springs
sparring at home

fans force fans cool their heels,
reels of celluloid heat the hall,
embraces taking their toll
on couples who've paid a high price
for hot collars under the impression
romance equals the cost of admission

air's been conditioned to squeeze
under doors when all floors sell out

sucking green lozenges, Mezzanine grows
hoarse from yelling "Whoa, Nelli" when
the deli downstairs offers to producers
its beet-colored candy buttons, while,
swimmingly, buttery pads attempt navigation
of the popcorn popper..but, pillars of salt halt
this dubious passage

National Pastime

Mickey Mantis, still as a stick
bent on preying, wet as sticky spit,
a skinny sinner, preaches a hungry shtick

knees locked,
unrepentant crowd-pleaser
in a pose reverential, concludes
morning's service in open-maw awe

full-on prayers for hysterical flies,
hearty gnats in party hats

an up-welling gusher of 'em

a buzzing, unmeteorological cloud..settling..

an arrowdite flight
streaking between pulpit
and home plate

MM licks clean digits and elbows
leaving no evidence of a feeding frenzy,
dismembered freight

What's Really Out There?

The Center for Derelict Satellites
announced its aversion to taking
up too much space

If the Milky Whey becomes genetically altered,
will the Kurds discard cheese altogether?

Meteors never shower if they think
the universe is looking

Does a comet scour and cleanse as
it plunges, then, vanishes?

With nothing left to notch, Van
Allen Belts tighten buckles

Ms Cosmic Raze is always searching
for cosmetics to mask hot flashes

Hubble huddles with black holes
hoping for clarity

Never fails..spacey matter
demanding time in the sun

20

Delicatessen

bone meets with blade,
meat purloined?

portions choice
whacked from
shoulders marbled

quarters cut
with sleek panache

elegant strokes, those..
the aneurysm knows

egos pitter patter and
hogs grow fatter

pork bellies under each arm,
though, my aversion to

saturated fats dangle from
any number of loose ends

prime rhyme depends
on hairy butchers who

badger well-fed poets leave their leanest cuts
next to the chops - scraps, on the saw-dusted floor

Saucy

tenderized, trimmed,
released from grommets circusy,
steaks sing the praises
of an out-of-tune
marinade unafraid
to serenade
this side of the beef,
bacon-wrapped,
bringer of grief

to cardiacs arrested
for disturbing the piece
of this leftover dish -
a vegetarian quiche -
bellyaching in a mush room
where gloom is dispersed
by a sous chef's broom

and, sauce, slowly stirred,
begins a beguine
in a slicksided tureen,
shimmies.. quakes..
then, a crossover dip
into a sexy Carioca,
perfect for a pair of
tipsy asparagus numb from
hanging a ride to Rio
with Ginger and Astaire

Rosetta..stoned

Egypt's crocodiles are in denial
hunters crave their skins

While awaiting delivery of her
Bulgari tiara, Fay Rowe offers to

lead a bull to the rushes
before returning to her rowing

now growing lats wide enough
to cast a shadow alongside Sphinx

conservative priests propose a limit
on visits to places with a car knock

as vibrations might cause temple
columns to collapse

In the midst of horseflies and pomp,
there goes Two Tank Amen filling up,

later, shifting to a lower gear to
gain traction in all that sand

Small Claims

The bed was a wetter's dream:
sheets, pileup of sweaty creases,
blanket, cloud cover that threatened
to suffocate summer's humid breath

The windowless wall
wailed through a vent
bent on scaring awake all snorers

I slipped on my boots,
stood again,
one hand holding my balls,
the other, a racket

and rode the ceiling fan
into every attic where
static was heard in a
number of pillow cases that
decided to settle out of court

Quebec

at the candy counter,
stuck on Lynn Oleum's
black and white squares,

there's Eddie,
budding cantor,
he of the throbbing heart,
with a can-do disposition,

counting Canadian coins
on the cusp of parity
with the sagging currency
south of the border

there go crinkly, discarded
cellophane wrappers and twisty ties
squealing their goodbyes as
floor corners the market on right
angles messing up their left turns

Eddie, crooning, pops off a toff,
skips down the road believing
there is no fissure he can't cross

Kitchen Capers

Celery, stalked by threatening corns
on the cob, slips on the linoleum
after Ms Chiquita went topless,
shagged in an energy shake, beets
staring although potatoes averted
their eyes

Kale and Cauliflower walk stalks
onto a magic carpet of peas
wave motion in a bird's eye,
past Wonderbread and Swiss
to Nockwurst and debris
while Kurds hang out at the corner
having skimmed the cream before sunrise,
while rude Abega tags along with the Greens
who leave the table without dressing

Celery, now stashed in the crisper
next to yells and a whisper,
awaits a dip in the sink's shallow end,
lifeguard wearing her avocado mask

Taking a Poll

I try to castanet over couples
flipping out over flamenco

heels stomp in the basement,
ballot boxes bouncing, heels stop on the
threshold of polling places where I scoop
up guts goats spew when ballots are through
being counted, counter fitters tallied by
hand, a Tallahassee tradition

Jim Crows flies over the Wisconsin Maid
cheese trail that Minnie and Winnie nibbled
enjoying views of each other on Lantern Lane
Hotel's veranda..Amanda, vain weather scout,
predicting rough wind ahead of rain

hurry, canes insist on tapping bottles
of beetles whose boring views on politics
grind to a halt..rose-tinted goggles not
quite the right prescription

SIDES

Pennies Pout, Dimes Dazzle

Quick, quack,
the quarter's back,
running out of room
on a field crowded with
change loose as a mascot moose
unsure of moves that qualify
as dimmer than all the switches
in coach's locked fuse box

Piggy backs
out of a flour sack,
shoulders a load squealing
louder than a stadium
high on radium fillings
with #2 coach drilling
his number one squad
on a series of strategies
which tickle the nickel
in donors' bequests -
pledged when their personal
goals were posted

TWA

With this sky cabin so crowded,
where will Gabriel lean a horn

Coats check their sleeves,
arms, standing at attention

Overhead, has-bins can be heard
crooning like Bobby Warin

False premise: upon landing,
all passengers with connecting
flights to remain seated if sated

If really hungry, all gaits are
encouraged by those deplaning

<u>Oh, tools</u>

injudicious
and bent on
avenging a
perceived wrong,

I found myself
at the docks,
midnight

careful to avoid
exposing my tool chest,
I maneuvered silently
under the yacht and
sank Timonious

__Pledge__

certain books give
me pained looks

as if their spines
recall vertebraying
like donkeys left
locked inside Lincolns,

studious Abe bends over
a table of contents,
polishing like mad

Brooks

compelled
to tote bags
shouldering snail mail
at this delivery stage,
the pony expresses
hoarse displeasure
whinnying snide remarks
to sidekicker
leathernecker
on alert for henchmen
kerchiefed and dangerous
especially when
saddles are blazing

Self-adhesive

After taking a severe licking,
stamp stumbled into a parcel post
whose only priority seemed to be
a question of sustaining verticality
ever since a nearby express window
of opportunity complained of
squeaky panes and a loose lock

Runner-Up

Eventually,
I whispered to the mare
my regret
for not
voting her into office

stalling,
at first,
to tickle both ears,
stroke that endearing muzzle,
massage flanks to

express my thanks
she hadn't dumped me
after the ballots were counted

Exhausted

if my bubblegum
wad plugs the
Cumberland Gap..

I Adirondack
to my Roledex..

remove all rocks
from Jackson Hole..

find a Schlage lock
my Okefenokee
will open..

if I learn to
fly in the ointment
without a co-pilot..

unzip the Zodiac..

maybe, then,
I'll get some sleep

EXTRA HELPINGS

<u>Corsair</u>

Harbor Cove 'round midnight..

all evening - rum royales
swallowed with a pirate's swagger
smuggling hints of bravado
into pockets of pants, mine,
that seemed to be a common
trysting place for treasure-
seeking hands, and, later,
when the bar was a boat
on choppy seas and, I, the
missing mate who kept falling
off the unsteady stool my legs
failed to wrap around, and,
when I couldn't pass, and,
nearly passed out, I knew
my gall was stoned, yes,
sloshed I was when the bar
turned tender and a voice
yelled, "Bellies Up",
I dragged my rum-ragged bottom
to the stern's gangplank
begging buddy

Al Coe haul my soggy ass home

Mastery of Subject

apothecarries
cash in apron pockets
deeper than a law suit

did e pluribus her unum,
practice malapropisms
without a poetic license

the flair of a Bunsen burner
dulls wayward gay blades
forcing barbers bearded
and cash-strapped, to teeter
on edges razor-thin hoping
daughters will trim and tidy
just the way they taught her

licensed by their learned schools,
somnambulists dabble in the occult,
a culture of second-guessing
market trends in which Mercedes
bends over backwards..a position
difficult to dam inflationary
currents swirling around
power and prestige

while, here, north of Topeka,
magician Merlin rolls up sleeves
and university degrees before
beginning field work as a farm assist

Still on Holiday, Cliche?

you never know
when or where
Bad Habit will bury
the hatchet and nemisis Nero
close the case on that
missing violin ever since
notes went out on strike
for recognition and a percent
of the prophets who
care not a sheckel
about who might cast
the first or last stone and
how far from shore it sails
before America's Cup
loses its handle..flails,
tips over spilling all
that sham bravado
and a case of Anchor Steams
into another turbulent
Sea of Dreams

Did You Phonious?

Bowie knifes through
the water like a speedboat
slicing into debris

on shore, a spoonbill,
gathering speed,
forks over a
picnic spread for four,
waders toe-scratching
orders in wet sand

early ibis in pearly vest,
chatter into morning's ear,
turning a deaf clef
into major thirds
other birds tune to
in hopes of joining
that avian choir
the phone company
strung wire glass
on which a middle C
pitch will sound

Pasties

in the past,
participles hung out with
verbs dangling from towers ivory, aloof,
capriciously washed away in a monsoon -
sooner or later about to blow

logic,
stirred into stew
the recipe for which peasants
found blooming in bracken,
was pooh-baahed by
Moravian philosophers
until all spicy debate
concluded in a slurp storm

pronouns,
known not to take a back seat
in cart or Corvette,
insinuated a slender influence
peppering documents
dear to folks
who believe all those tales
about good giving evil
the slam

Buenos Dias

I did not pick Chapultapec
out of just any pack, señor.
Nervous and blindfolded,
jaguar piñata and I trade blows
and cell phone numbers,
call in a split decision, then, pose
for photographs while tour guide
Luiz is pleased to hand out
bus passes to travelers
not booking burros or
sitting on their asses

Will our taxi to Zacatecas
take us past the silver mine
expecting a spring polish
even though undergrads with a
sterling reputation might hop
off and on their study van
lingering longer over fermentation
vats than it takes to analyze
the local Corona

Tired, dehydrated,
smelling salsa and corn tortillas,
we lunch at Cantina Rowena,
a bunch of campers happy
our dictionaries are in Spanish
and Aguascalientes's Best Western's
best rates are exclusively for
the guest snorkel dressed in

wet suit, face mask, fins

Flora Boradora

Daisy fields a fly ball

Meadow, covered in dirt,
welcomes Tide up her skirt

fast-falling sky,
no parachute

shot of Four Roses, too many shots
and Colt forgets to shoot the piano player
who left her keys under collapsed blue tent

movements cramped, yet, Daisy turns in her
glove inhaling sweaty leather and tempo
changes reflecting a rereading of isobars

barkeeper tied
to his true calling -
hauling fertilizer to any number
of patches wet

for those plucking daisy petals,
the piano's ivories' haunting refrain:

I love you,
I love you not

Serious Footage

into the frame
Odessa steps,
flat-footed female
in fitted Ferragamo
rushin' to join
several photo shoots
hot on the trail
of Turkmenistani
Rocky Steppes,
notable national
filmmaker, poet,
in cahoots with
"Razors of the
Living Dead" on
this, their final
tour before going
underground

Somersaulted

past fall, losing its balance,
toppling hills of beans
the brothers roasted
while cameramen boasted
of filming java steaming
from a million coffee mugs

somersaulted, avoiding,
by a whirlwind's sudden shift,
Tourette's syndrome
under contract as a
temporary caravansary
for overactive dromedaries,
for overheated desert shoots,
Arabica beans, high-priced extras

windmilling, somersaulted
tumbling into winter's most
risky snow bank
(underwriter for low-budget sagas),
flakes uninsured,
though FDI sees to it
that the season, for savers
and sippers, is most jolly

Geosynchroneous

An expert in African morays, Rivu lets
pachyderms pack tantamounts, testaments,
wiffle bells and kells into elegant trunks
apt to turn up noses at last year's model
stitched under the Tuscan son's demanding
eye the storm of which could be a danger
to contract's clauses, siesta's snores,
and, of course, trunks' shipping dates,
medjools more than satisfactory for
Turkish vendors, Italian scooters' fenders
that feud with iconoclastic revelers
besotted and beside themselves conspicuous
in attire (oh, thank you, Malay rubber
workers), the boss for us obliged to share
several sets of scandals - Interpol
perfectly willing to try on sandals
themselves having second thoughts
about exposing so many nails, flathead and
pointy toe, to hammerhead sharks ready to
strike a blow for world peace.

Astragalus

in that magical realm,
Tarsus Territory,
held in exalted esteem,
none exceeds Phalange,
hermaphroditic wizard,
ruler of the Incli Nation

who walks a fine line
between subjects
bearing a propensity
to grin and bear it,
while others grimace,
stew with carrot

alarmed the Nation's soles
are flat on their backs,
toes hammerheaded,
plainly out of joint,

wizard mixes potions
containing portions of
olibanum, myosin,
Eucalyptus gum,

rendering obsolete
all previous ministrations, thus,
eliminating warts, bunions, corns

and planting in all plantars
the desire for perfection
of form and function,
so, once again,
dancing and joyous leaping
be prevalent throughout the land

Comb Home

Let us pray Toupee
and best friend Wiggy,
after a series of
hair-raising auditions,
finally get the part

Wheat slices lie comatoast
corner-cut on a bald pate,
butter spreads out on the bed,
while, after cudding classes,
a herd of cows, all hard of hearing,
choose to join a lactator's local

And, jam..anybody in some?
I open both lids and apricops
south of Solvang police every gate
left ajar when the Masons departed

In my decaffeinated confusion,
coffee does appear to percolate
for that Columbian donkey,
and, with it, I unlock the dough box,
nuts and bolts of any budget especially
one where brioche is flown in from
the Paris Hilton

After Graduation

it seemed like earth tilted a few (advanced) degrees

making an educated guess, a freshman flock of
European tits settled under eaves

student union's bowling alley declared a strike

public address system, eschewing dresses, began
wearing Lee's jeans and leather boots

elements in chemistry's lab figured they'd polish
periodic tables

Keg partied with Lager and Ale over the county line

grass, left uncut, made for a smelly smoke

flower beds changed all sheets..pillow cases
ending up in a lawyer's brief

spirit of knowledge imparted bemoans the multitude
of empty classrooms

student records are mailed out in vinyl format
complete with sleeve and button cuff

Raked

orchestra's got plenty of
wrong notes to worry about

expensive boxes know
when not to box, when
to set aside gloves,
a mouth piece

dress circle
slips into something
more comfortable,

balcony leans forward,
pretends hard of hearing

in the last row,
aknackRownisms
agree on a timely
replacement,

nod a collective "Yes"
believing contoured seats

convey sober comfort
to anatomical anomalies
mezzanine misanthropes
resolve to regiment

"Avoid improbabilities
inherent in a/sym/met/ries
desperate to assimilate,"
cautions railing,

holding on to
rational
brass,

a Tijuana tradition

Cone Zone

Nervous Aorta looks sorta lost,
leaving her ventricle muddling
in the middle of rush-hour traffic,
radiator taking a leak,
bypass valves sneaking a peek

Her bare feet skip over
plaque set in cement meant for
dentists, chewers of sugarless gum,
who give eyeteeth 20/20 supervision
in case clots close arteries
to laughter's one-way out

Air, coppery, conductive, pulses
a steady heat beat, heat beat,
pumps mutter a sympathetic
dubglub dubglub..while
Carbon Miranda waits for rude,
but, rich producer R.U. Mangosteen
to champion her plugs

on the set,
Ms Cochita bets Guff the gaffer
that bananas will unzip their
jackets offering small bites
to big mouths, maws unaware
that well-marked crosswalks backward
into the heart of the matter

__Maxilla__

Expholee ate fried chicken steak
still stuck on Trevor's tee

spoon shoveled potatoes, mashed,
resembling this season's slushly snow

knife, serrated, opened a peas package
shocked at the crowded conditions on
arriving gravy trains

fork scolded rude abegas for departing
wilted salads without even dressing

dissolving peptides gurglegasp, then,
wash back to clear Expholee's pipeline
beginning to back up

in the barking lot, exchanging a leather
leash for a little longer lease,

Expholee's Aunt Acid threw up her hands
when a Pomeranian leaped for those Nipples
of Venus suddenly scooped outta sight via
nimble, thimble-fingered Rapper Cellophane,
and, ducking to avoid rapping the roof of
her mouth, leggy consonants crouch, yell
"Yipee, yahoo" and boogie saliva's surf

shushing past reticent Port Wisdom
to the loquacious Canine Coast

Whirled Series

catcher holds his breath above his head,
a 3 count needed to begin the game

breathing down batters' necks, smelling
odors aromatic, hardballs take aim at
sweaty pitchers of minty lemonade

a series of pitches seriously refreshing,
each more tangy than a baseline drive

raise the level of thirst that cursed
the worst players stuck in fields
parched of dreams

boyish, straining faces dash past bases
to dig the dugout from under mounds of mints

box offices feel the force as fans
whip up a currency commotion,
every denomination worthy of account

owners expect to collect, especially
if bleachers are fully loaded

Malta

Beajolais
exhausted beside Gamay,
his label peeled exposing
a sleek underbelly not unlike
her latest platter of salmon
jelly fishing for compliments
after corks popped up infatuated
with a rustic bouquet, quite
possibly, Iberian, half-buried on
tongues tired of licking their chops

trumpeter, plastered,
takes a swan dive
off a shipwreck,
casks barreling out of the hold
unions thirst fore and aft,

mates, medicated, materialize
on crane's steel brow,
tunnel Astaspumante
down a ferrous funnel
whose neck never knew
a gag from a gaggle

Pica Pica

juggling rolling pins, Pam-slick pans,
loaflovers, exuberant flour-sifters,
flap flower-pattern aprons

flip-off measuring spoons dizzy spinning bowls,
wave rubber spatulas layering ingredients in
proportions outlandish yielding loaves enough
to double-deck the Earl of Sandwich his
habit-forming hold-the-mayo ham 'n cheese

out of thornbread's prickly crust
arise squally birds, cries raucous in
avian thirds held nestbound by umbilical
chords wound around feathered necks next of kin

Batterup,
our workstation's only pitcher,
throws down the gauntlet spilling so much
ill will on magpies' meringue glacé,

that, in a flurry of feathers,
they flock to Carlotta's Used Car Lot
pecking at the Packard Clipper's
split naugahyde..

cozy quarters if you like downhome grub
battered 'n spice fried crisp in one hand,
beer, in the other

Declaimers

Shirley, you recall reading
about Visigoths and Huns, those
often surly thespians whose
winning ways brought down the
house (actually, all of them),
and, who, then, passed the hat
(usually, with head attached),
before marching on to wow the
crowds at the next venue

how and why, versed in bellicosity,
prone to bellowing vile utterances,
they were waved at politely,
shoo, shooed along bloody roadsides
by certain citizens still left standing
 (next to those who were not) who
wasted no time booking accommodations
in sunny Catania or Crete

Styrofoam

hiccups north of state line
last a whole lot longer if
you don't Handel the chorus

this jump is jointin'..
thin-fingered singers
thread their bobbins,
a ton of tenors, adjustin' cords,
grab fer Java, jostle, high seas
spillin' over the rim

couple of joints conduct their own
slow passage, measure success by inhalin'

sittin' on the mezz,
soprano sips tea,
gazes down on basses -
collars up, backin' into places
she's aware fit kinda tight

conversation sparks animation
without muddyin' waters which is
a big help to staff keepin' ears clean,
all the better to listen fer sharps 'n flats

why, just this mornin',
fer singin' down low,
two contraltos were evicted
from one

Organic

how could the shoe
store's inventory
be missing a pear

in the sauna,
bananas slip outta
their jackets

solving theft of fruit
in Solvang means
calling in the apricops

between her breasts,
silence of the yams

no matter the
color of skins,
berries do date,
they just canteloupe

on her boutique farm,
cousin Tiffani
begins harvesting
baby carats today

Tabbytown

furballed, yet, feisty,
this whiskery jurisdiction
admits to a paw city
of leaders,
so, Cat Apult
claws her way
past the litter box
to the Liter Lounge

there, behind the bar,
a dispensary for the
magical "meow sequence",
which, if uttered with
purrsistent purring and
intermittent catcalls,
bestows upon
the successful feline

the mickey of stretch..
the mantle of mayor..
the caliph of catnip..

titles notarized
to notify all parties
that this town is
open for business

and all kats hip
to the snip-snap
rap of tender tip tap, tap
letting all quadripeds
(on or off their meds)
know there's no crisis
of confidence here..

why, this place is
categorized

<u>Towing Toto</u>

the yellow brick rode into a cul-de-sac,
suburban descendent of the sack of Rome
by hordes ready to rumble,
even stumble over stones
upended that pretended a stance
egalitarian under this 4am
KC flapjack moon

perspiring roads, empty, now, of purpose
and preference of destination,

cheer the arrival of Rhodes, Cecil,
relentless adventurer, seeker of
mothers' loads upon his back he'd carry

a legal coupling he'd consider
to keep his name from gossiping
the KC columns -

those pillars of society that
never bear accusations of verticality
lying down

Pons

some nerve -
a ganglion roars,
mane stuck between doors
of the last synapse
to Medulla Oblongata

along the tracks,
Brain waves to crowds
eating their hartzout
while onions elope with a liver

some spine -
resolve melting like butter
pads skating on thin dice
thrown into a yonder
wild and blue

a fate
fortune never forgets,
memory a safe deposit box
contents never emptied

is blood a navigable river

Dillydally

Archimedes
waits at Deedees
for just desserts
in slinky skirts

calculus of charm
invented to disarm
scientific minds
attentive to behinds

loaves or fishes
not his dishes,
he'll calculate
her measured gait

say something cute,
then, square the root
of her hypotenuse..
back in Syracuse

__Undaunted__

Aristotle
hits the bottle,
a practice shot
in the parking lot

reverberates,
he contemplates
his anger spent,
he'll circumvent

public dismay,
quit the NRA,
grow short his hair,
end the affair

with bloated fame,
reclaim his name -
mass debater,
instigator

<u>1947</u>

Roswell plays itself - sceptic tanks
think they're losin' it when flushed
with a chemical stink..helium liftin'
everybody's spirits everyday 'cept
Sunday when somebody's lord plays
host to wavers 'n wafers that stay
suspended on tongues too tongue-tied
to admit that the collared crowd lied..
hard to get flags wavin' when coyote
nabs pal breeze 'n truth's up for
grabs when alien convention tents get
pitched..believers let their eyes scan
the skies..heat waves suck air out of
wind stealer's jaws, believers find
relief sippin' sodas outta straws..
Roswell, don't go bellyachin' - buttons
your vendors sell by the hundreds every
day 'cept Sunday when banks close and
closets open doors to local ETs and their
uncles and their aunts..let scorpions
dance on heat-seekin' rocks..did then,
will again..that's Roswell, playin' host
to a hundred versions of the truth.

CLEAN-UP

The author of **Picnic Poetry** wishes to thank his wonderful
short story writer friend Mary O'Toole for her humor, patience
and discerning eye in assisting me in a myriad of positive ways
in the production of this paperback book. She is the author of
A Little Bite And Other Stories which is available as an e-book
and as a paperback book.

The author acknowledges the consistent 'helpings' of practical
advice and support offered over the years by fellow San Francisco
First Saturday Pocket Poets writers Nancy Wakeman, Jane Rades,
Susan Swan, Marvin R. Hiemstra and Al Averbach.

And, as inspiring 'word warrior' and mentor, the author is grateful
for the contribution of Fiona Page.

Also, a special 'shout out' to graphic designer Danielle Jackson
for her dedication and knowledge in the completion of this project.

Now, to you, readers hungry for the good stuff, who have enjoyed
picnic portions unexpectedly filling, sides and even extra helpings
or the entire picnicable spread before you, your poet provisioner
says 'Thanks for the chow down'.

stephen.kopel@live.com

www.ingramcontent.com/pod-product-compliance
Lightning Source LLC
Chambersburg PA
CBHW071830020426
42331CB00007B/1679